IS IT ALWAYS RIGHT TO BE RIGHT?

A Tale of Transforming Workplace Conflict into
Creativity and Collaboration

Warren H. Schmidt
BJ Gallagher Hateley

Illustrations by Sam Weiss

AMACOM
American Management Association
New York • Atlanta • Boston • Chicago • Kansas City • San Francisco • Washington, D.C.
Brussels • Mexico City • Tokyo • Toronto

Special discounts on bulk quantities of AMACOM books are available to corporations, professional associations, and other organizations. For details, contact Special Sales Department, AMACOM, a division of American Management Association, 1601 Broadway, New York, NY 10019.
Tel.: 212-903-8316.   Fax: 212-903-8083.
Web site: www. amacombooks.org

This publication is designed to provide accurate and authoritative information in regard to the subject matter covered. It is sold with the understanding that the publisher is not engaged in rendering legal, accounting, or other professional service. If legal advice or other expert assistance is required, the services of a competent professional person should be sought.

Library of Congress Cataloging-in-Publication Data

Schmidt, Warren H.
     Is it always right to be right? : a tale of transforming workplace conflict into creativity and collaboration / Warren H. Schmidt, B.J. Gallagher Hatley ; illustrations by Sam Weiss.
          p. cm.
     Using Schmidt's earlier work of the same title as a model.
     Includes biolographical references.
     ISBN 0-8144-7095-5
     1. Conflict management. 2. Teams in the workplace. I. Hateley, B.J. Gallagher. II. Weiss, Sam. III. Title.

HD42 .S34 2001
658.4'053—dc21

                                                                                2001022269

Printing number

10 9 8 7 6 5 4 3 2 1

We dedicate this book to those who have

the patience to listen,

the courage to be forthright,

and

the wisdom to create new pathways to peace.

Preface

The fall of 1969 was a time of great turmoil and divisiveness in America. The controversy over the war in Vietnam was raging. Blacks were serving — and dying — in disproportionate numbers, and tensions between the races were high. There was a growing "generation gap" between younger and older Americans. The Women's Liberation Movement was just beginning.

October 15 was designated "Vietnam Moratorium Day" — and Americans were asked to pause and reflect on what was happening to our country. I woke up at 5:00 A.M., and began to write about a land where everyone was right and no one would ever admit they might be wrong. It was a simple parable that wrote itself once it was begun.

The *Los Angeles Times* printed this parable on the front page of its Opinion section on Sunday, November 9, 1969, under the headline "Is It Always Right to Be Right?" This triggered a wide range of reactions — many individual responses (including letters from Senator Edward Kennedy and Vice President Spiro Agnew), a reprint in *The Congressional Record*, and an animated film narrated by Orson Welles. The film won an Academy Award as the "Best Animated Short Subject" of 1971. Since then, the film — and video — have been used in conferences and training programs throughout the world.

Exactly thirty years later — in November, 1999 — BJ Gallagher Hateley (my frequent coauthor) suggested that we write a book about conflict in organizaions using the "Always

Right" parable as a model. She, Sam Weiss, and I had just completed work on a book and video dealing with stereotyping (*Pigeonholed in the Land of Penguins*). Adrienne Hickey, executive editor of AMACOM Books, and her colleagues liked the idea. The result is what you are holding in your hand.

During the writing and illustrating of this book, BJ, Sam, and I had a few disputes ourselves. In the process, we rediscovered that it is easier to write about conflict than to manage it. But because we have deep and caring relationships (and because we *do try* to practice what we preach), the disputes were settled, the manuscript was produced, and our friendship remains intact. I am grateful to my colleagues for giving a "second life" to a very old parable with a message that is timeless.

BJ, Sam, and I hope that the reading of this little book will be both enjoyable and useful — and that you will be better able to deal with people who are very certain that they are right and you are wrong . . . .

Warren H. Schmidt

PART ONE

There once was an organization

where people were always right.

They knew they were right . . .

. . . and they were proud of it.

It was a place where people stated with confidence,

"I am right and you are wrong."

These were

words of

conviction,

courage,   strength,

and moral certainty.

No one was ever heard to say,

"I might be wrong"

or

"Perhaps I've misjudged."

Nor would anyone say,

"You might be right"

or

"Perhaps you have a point there."

For these were words of weakness,

doubt,

cowardice,

and moral ambiguity.

When differences arose

among the people of this organization . . .

They looked not for Truth,

but for confirmation

of what they already believed.

When differences arose

between management

and employees,

management would say:

"We have worked hard

and made many sacrifices

to build

this great and prosperous organization.

"We are the envy of other enterprises,

for we are strong and powerful.

"Our success is built on solid values:

    return on investment,

    profitability,

    shareholder value,

    and global competitiveness.

"The proof of our success

is everywhere to see:

Look at our stock rating,

⠀⠀⠀⠀our influence and prestige,

⠀⠀⠀⠀⠀⠀our market share.

"Look at the high standing

⠀⠀⠀we enjoy in our industry.

"We don't understand you employees today —

your chronic complaints,

your values and work habits,

your unwillingness to sacrifice for the organization.

"Why are you employees

so unhappy —

so ungrateful?"

Management was right, of course,

and they knew it.

But the employees of the organization would respond:

"We are unhappy with good reason.

"We see a place

where greed and selfishness

are the order of the day . . .

". . . a place where *looking* good is more important

than *being* good

or *doing* good.

"Management proclaims that

    'People are our most important resource' —

    but reality does not match your rhetoric.

"You are interested only in profits,

    not people.

"You have sold your souls

    to Wall Street,

        and you worship at the altar

            of short-term profits.

"How can you expect us

to be loyal to you

and to work hard

    just so you can get your bonuses?"

The employees were right, of course,

and they knew it.

And the gap between management and employees

grew wider . . .

and deeper . . . .

When differences arose

between people of different colors,

those of one color would say:

 "We have worked for many years

to create an organization of fairness and equity

for *all* our people.

"We have come a long way

since our early days,

and we have made much progress.

Anyone who is objective would agree that

work life is better than ever.

"Just look how much
people of *all* colors
have achieved.

"Opportunity is abundant
as never before.

"We've promoted you,
given you recognition,
and more responsibility . . . .

"Why aren't you grateful

and content with your success?"

These people were right, of course,

and they knew it.

But those of other colors would reply:

"The progress you speak of
is too little,
too late.

"You say that you value diversity,

but hollow tokenism is all that we see.

"Our training is inferior,

our pay inadequate,

and we are too often treated

as second-class citizens.

"The playing field is still not level . . . and so many doors

remain closed to us.

"While blatant racism

has often been addressed,

the subtler hurts persist —

eroding our spirits,

impeding our progress.

"How can you expect us to be content

when we still have so far to go?"

These people were right, of course,

and they knew it.

And the gaps between people of different colors

grew wider . . .

and deeper . . . .

When differences arose

between the departments,

people of one department would say:

"Our way is the right way.

" *We're* the ones

who do all the work around here.

"You are just overhead —

you don't pull your weight.

"If it weren't for us,

    this place would be history.

"We're in charge for good reason—

we are the smart ones,

with talent and skill.

"Stop your complaining,

get with the program,

and work like a team . . .

or we'll find someone who will."

These people were right, of course,

and they knew it.

But the people of other departments would reply:

"We beg to differ . . . .

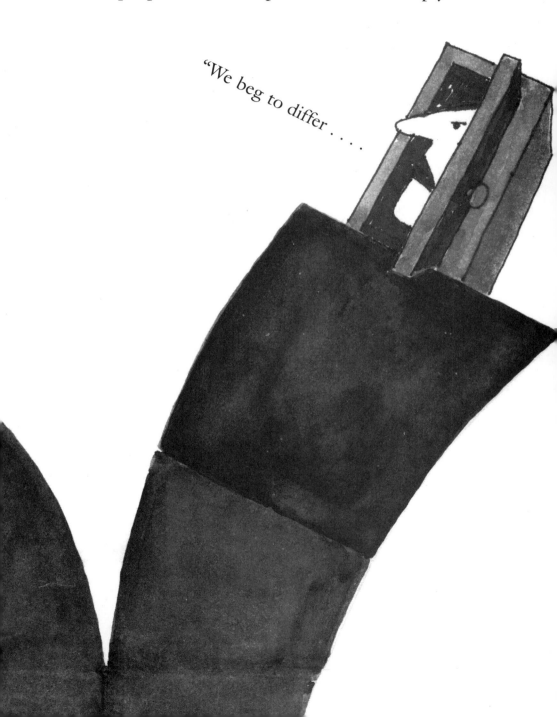

"You strut your big egos,

you bully and bellow;

you use your clout

to try to make us comply.

"*We* know who really makes things work around here . . . .

You'd be in deep trouble

without our support.

"*You* are the ones who are mistaken.

You should appreciate *us*.

"Who processes the paper?

Who makes the work flow smoothly?

Who crosses the t's and dots the i's?

Who sees to quality and

maintains standards?

These people were right, of course,

and they knew it.

And the gaps between the departments

grew wider . . .

and deeper . . . .

When differences arose

between men and women,

the men would say:

"We have spent our lives sacrificing and building our careers.

"We have climbed to the top through hard work and determination.

"We know how to work as a team,

we don't whine and complain . . . .

"If you want equal treatment,

then act more like us.

"We treat you with respect,

and we've opened up opportunity,

but don't expect to get more than you earn."

These men were right, of course,

and they knew it.

But the women would say:

"We are tired of waiting and paying our dues.

We've been in the pipeline too long,

working and waiting for our reward . . . .

"We see no light at the end of the tunnel.

"We work and we work,

    only to hit our heads

    on a shatter-proof glass ceiling.

"When we try to be like you,

we get labeled as too aggressive;

and when we soften our style

we're seen as too weak.

"We're damned if we do,

and damned if we don't.

"This is a game we never can win."

These women were right, of course,

and they knew it.

And the gap between the genders

grew wider . . .

and deeper . . . .

And so it went in this organization . . . .

Group after group defined the *right*,

and took a stand against those who opposed them.

It happened between the superstars

who flaunted their achievements,

and those who were the also-rans,

regarded as "not leadership material."

It happened between the futurists

who urged, "Faster, faster,"

and the traditionalists

who pleaded, "Let's not abandon our roots."

It happened between the hi-tech people

who said, "Technology will liberate us,"

and the hi-touch people

who said, "Technology is killing our souls."

Everyone was right, of course,

and they knew it.

And *all* the gaps grew . . .

w i d e r . . .

and

deeper . . . .

. . . until finally one day . . .

. . . all interaction

and activity

ground to a halt.

Each group stood firm in their "rightness,"

glaring with proud eyes

at those too blind to see The Truth.

They were determined

to maintain their positions at all costs —

    for this is essential when you are right.

No one traveled across the many gaps.

    No one talked to those on other sides.

    No one listened.

Everyone was frozen in their rightness.

Life became cold and lonely,

with everyone so isolated.

People were resentful and angry.

Random acts of sabotage occurred.

Their place of work grew grim and gray . . . .

Then . . . one day,

a strange new sound

was heard in the organization . . . .

"Uh, maybe I was wrong,"

someone said softly.

A collective gasp of disbelief

was heard throughout

the organization.

How could anyone say such a crazy thing?

They thought they must be hearing things.

"Perhaps you were right after all,"

      someone else said quietly.

The people looked around to see

who could be uttering such nonsense.

They laughed at the stupidity and weakness of such words.

But the voices persisted . . .

talking back and forth,

each exploring the other's point of view.

And after a while,

    some of the people began to listen . . . .

They listened with uncertainty at first,

unaccustomed as they were

to hearing new words

from new voices.

They listened carefully;

they listened with reservations.

But they listened.

And as they listened,

    they were surprised

        as they discovered things in common

            they had not known before.

And as they *listened* anew,

they began to *see* anew . . .

. . . seeing fellow workers and good people

where they once had seen only adversaries

Here and there,

    people joined together

    to act upon

    their newly discovered common interests . . . .

Creative projects blossomed throughout the enterprise.

With each new joint effort,

　　people's trust in one another grew . . .

. . . along with their hopes for the future.

They developed a new confidence in their ability
to shape their own destiny . . .

. . . *together.*

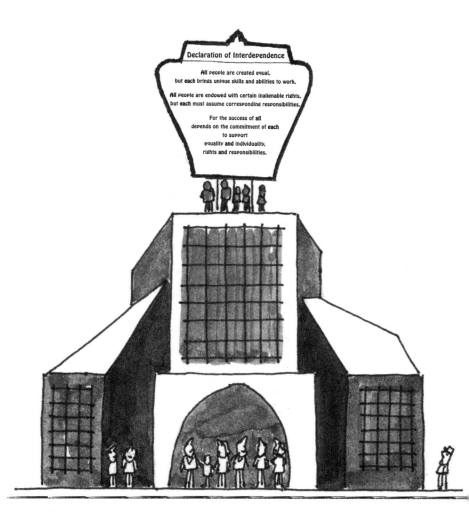

They stated their new beliefs

in a "Declaration of Interdependence . . ."

Declaration of Interdependence

All people are created equal,
but **each** brings unique skills and abilities to work.

All people are endowed with certain inalienable rights,
but **each** must assume corresponding responsibilities.

For the success of **all**
depends on the commitment of **each**
to support
equality **and** individuality,
rights **and** responsibilities.

In this organization,

people had learned how two rights

can make a serious wrong.

They saw how *little* courage it takes
to point the finger of blame . . .

. . . and how *much* courage it takes
to extend the hand of partnership.

And they realized how *little* wisdom there is

in defending a narrow right . . .

. . . and how *much* wisdom there is

in seeking a broader understanding.

Most important of all,

the people of this organization had learned

that the quest for Truth is never over . . .

and the challenge is always the same:

To stop fighting long enough to listen . . . .

To learn from others who differ . . . .

To try new approaches and take new risks . . . .

To seek out and build new relationships . . . .

. . . And to keep working at a process

that never ends . . . .

Declaration of Interdependence

All people are created equal,
but each brings unique skills and abilities to work.

All people are endowed with certain inalienable rights,
but each must assume corresponding responsibilities.

For the success of all
depends on the commitment of each
to support
equality and individuality,
rights and responsibilities.

THE END OF THE STORY

(. . . the beginning of the future?)

PART TWO

Tips and Tools for Dealing with Differences

Conflicts in organizations are inevitable. People bring their unique perspectives and interests to the workplace. They have different priorities, and deal with different parts of the tasks to be done and the goals to be achieved. Conflicts bring these differences into focus — and can lead to either positive or negative results.

In some ways *CONFLICT* parallels the Chinese ideograph for *CRISIS*:

Danger　　*Opportunity*

Conflict changes things for the better or the worse — <u>depending on how it is managed.</u>

The pages that follow suggest some things to consider when you become involved in a conflict as a "combatant" or a "third party."

Contents

Where You Sit (Often) Determines Where You Stand
(The Role of Position in Conflict)

Conflicts are a normal occurrence in organizations. Some studies have shown that top managers spend about 25 percent of their time dealing with conflicts of one kind or another, and middle managers spend even more time in conflict. In deciding what kinds of conflicts to depict in our parable, we asked several management seminar groups what kinds of conflicts are most common.

Conflicting Groups in the "Right" Parable

Management
"We have worked hard . . . to build this great and prosperous organization."

Employees
"We see a place where greed and selfishness are the order of the day."

People of One Color
"We have come a long way . . . ."

People of Other Colors
"The playing field is still not level . . . ."

Line Departments
"We're the ones who do all the work . . . . you are just overhead . . . ."

Staff Departments
"We know who really makes things work around here . . . ."

Men
"We have climbed to the top through hard work and determination."

Women
"We are tired of waiting and paying our dues . . . . We work and we work, only to hit our heads on a shatter-proof glass ceiling."

Futurists
"Faster, faster."

Traditionalists
"Let's not abandon our roots"

"Hi-Tech" People
"Technology will liberate us."

"Hi-Touch" People
"Technology is killing our souls."

Other organizational groups that have different responsibilities and status — and therefore naturally develop their own preceptions of procedures, opportunities, and what is "realistic" and "fair":

Supervisors vs. Workers
Salaried Workers vs. Hourly Workers
Designers or Engineers vs. Manufacturers
Salespersons vs. Producers
Customers vs. Clerks
Salespeople vs. Customer Service People
Suppliers/Vendors vs. Users
Headquarters vs. Branch (Field) Staff

What groups have you seen in conflict?

_____ vs. _____

_____ vs. _____

_____ vs. _____

_____ vs. _____

_____ vs. _____

_____ vs. _____

_____ vs. _____

_____ vs. _____

_____ vs. _____

_____ vs. _____

_____ vs. _____

_____ vs. _____

_____ vs. _____

_____ vs. _____

_____ vs. _____

_____ vs. _____

Helpful Words in a Discussion of Differences

The words we use in a dispute are critically important. They can inflame and confuse *or* they can clarify and invite dialogue. Here are some helpful words and phrases to include in your vocabulary when you are engaged in a conflict situation.

- "We both seem to want . . . ."

- "Let me see if I understand what you are saying . . . [and then repeat or rephrase what you think you just heard]."

- "Let's look at what might happen if we adopted your proposal . . . and then let's do the same with my proposal . . . ."

- "Let's be clear on the outcomes we would like to achieve . . . ."

- "Who else besides us has something at stake in what we are discussing?"

- "Who else might shed some light on this?"

- "Who might help us discuss our differences?"

- "I could support what you propose if ...."

- "Under what circumstances could you support what I am proposing?"

- "We both seem to agree on X, but we have different views on Y...."

- "Is there any additional information or other points of view that would be helpful to us?"

- "You seem to be saying, '[State what you think was said]' .... Is that right?"

Words that Escalate a Conflict
("Fighting Words")

We have all witnessed (and participated in) discussions of differences where the conflict between people escalates and the chances for agreement diminishes. **Much of this happens because of the words we use.**

Here are some phrases to **avoid** if you want to find a peaceful and creative resolution:

- "The trouble with you is . . . ."

- "How can anyone who is as smart as you claim to be really believe . . . ?"

- "Where did you get that (stupid/crazy/silly) idea anyway?"

- "When you get a little more information and a better perspective we can talk . . . ."

- "That's a dumb idea."

- "Are you SERIOUS?"

- "I understand your point . . . but let me tell you what *really* happened."

- "You are just plain wrong."

- "You always . . . ."

- "You never . . . ."

- "How can you say that?"

- "You're kidding . . . ."

- "You *can't* be serious."

- "Any idiot can see that . . . ."

- "You don't honestly believe that, do you?"

- "Don't B.S. me."

- "I can't believe you said that."

- *"What were you thinking?"*

Add your own (the words that turn you off in a conflict):

_____

_____

_____

_____

_____

_____

_____

_____

The Conflict Management Continuum
(A Systematic Way to View and Approach a Conflict)

Once underway, conflicts often escalate and widen. What begins as a simple disagreement over facts can broaden (and intensify) into personal attacks that make both parties defensive and unable to deal with the original disagreement.

One way to avoid this is to have a *mental map* of conflict — a systematic way to determine what kind of conflict you are dealing with. Here is such map showing and defining four points that conflict may be about:

Facts — what each party believes is an accurate description of the present situation

Methods — what actions each party believes should be taken

Goals — what each party believes should be achieved

Values — the long-term issues that are at stake

A conflict could be over one or any combination of these.

Because emotions easily and quickly become involved in a conflict discussion, it is useful to have a strategy — a systematic way of looking at differences and how they can be understood and managed.

This instrument is designed to help you to understand your own approach to conflict — and to suggest a road map for behaving in a way that can increase the possibility of reducing the destructive "noise" that occurs in most conflict situations.

It will not guarantee an elegant solution to any given conflict — but it *will* give you a systematic way of handling your part of a conflict discussion.

Basic Behaviors in a Conflict Discussion:

Telling and Persuading — expressing what you see as the facts of the situation, their significance, your proposal for dealing with them, and the outcomes you believe should be achieved. Your goal is to get the other party to understand and accept this same perspective, and reach the same conclusion.

Listening and Learning — getting a clear understanding of the other party's perception of the facts, actions to take, and goals to achieve. Your goal is to be certain that you have an accurate and clear understanding of what the other party believes and wants.

Exploring, Creating, Negotiating, and Compromising — discovering and enlarging areas of agreement between you and the other party — and maintaining your relationship so that your common interests can be advanced.

The Conflict Management Continuum

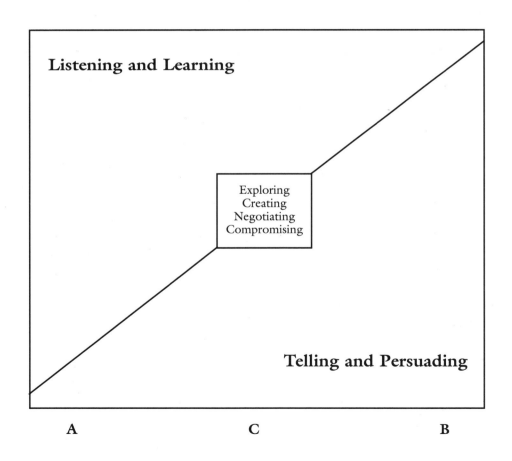

Behaviors That Can Move Conflict toward Creative Problem-Solving

A. Listening and Learning

Communication is usually the first casualty in conflict discussions. Each party is impatient and doesn't want to listen to a point of view that is so clearly wrong. Rather than listening, each is preparing a response while the other party is talking. *You can break this unproductive process by simply listening.* By good listening, you can break the cycle. Some suggestions:

Listen actively.
Check your understanding: "Let me see if I understand you. Are you saying that [and then repeat your understanding of what you have just heard]?"

Ask questions for clarification.
"Could you go over that last point again? I'm not sure I fully understand it."

Probe for primary motivations and concerns.
"What do you see as the most important issue at stake here — and why do you feel so strongly about it?"

Probe for secondary and less obvious motivations and concerns.
"Are there other reasons this is important to you?"

Probe for areas of uncertainty and openings for influence and change.
"Are there any aspects of this issue that still puzzle you?"

Summarize the other party's perception of the facts.
"Tell me if I have a correct understanding of how you see this situation." And then give your summary of the other's perception of the facts.

Summarize the other party's recommendations for action.
"Tell me if this is what you are proposing." And then give your summary of what the other party is proposing.

Summarize the other party's goals.
"Is this what you want to achieve?" And then give your perception of the other party's goals.

Summarize the other party's stated and implied values.
"If I understand you correctly, you believe that your approach to this problem is important because in the long run it will . . . ."

B. Telling and Persuading

State your own perception of the facts and the basis for them.
"Here is how I see what is going on — and what I'm basing it on."

State your own recommendations for action and their justification.
"Here is what I propose — and why I think it makes sense."

State your own goals and why they are important.
"Here is what I hope will come out of this — regardless of whose approach we follow. I think we must keep our eye on these hoped-for outcomes: [then state them]. What do you think?"

State your own goals (hoped-for outcomes) and whether they are the same or different from the other party's stated or implied goals.
"The things I hope will come out of this are . . . . Are these the same goals you have in mind? If so, let's think about the various ways we might accomplish them."

Speculate on the cause of the differences, and invite a response.
"I wonder why we want such different things. Do you have any idea?"

State how the proposed goals are consistent or inconsistent with agreed-upon values.
"Since we both seem to share the same values, wouldn't it make sense to . . . ?"

State your own values and how they underlie the goals you are proposing.
"I think you know that I feel strongly about [these values] . . . . That's why I am attracted to . . . ."

Underscore the importance of these values.
"I think we can both agree that whatever we decide to do, we must choose actions and goals that are consistent with these values."

Invite the other party to reconsider his or her position — and how he or she would be advantaged by this.
"I wish you would be willing to take another look at what you have been proposing. It would take a good bit of courage to do this, but I think you would feel better."

C. Exploring, Creating, Negotiating, and Compromising

State where both sets of perception of the *facts* are the same or different.
"I think that we both *agree* that . . . . We disagree about . . . . You perceive X, while I perceive Y . . . ."

Speculate on the cause of the differences — and invite a response.
"I wonder if the reason we see things differently is because . . . . Why do you think we have such different views about what happened?"

State where both sets of *goals* are the same or different.
"You seem to want a different outcome from what I do. If I understand you correctly, you want X, and I want Y."

Speculate on why the differences might exist.
"My hunch is that we have arrived at different views because . . . . Why do you think we see things so differently?"

State your own recommendations for *action* — and the justification for them.
"I strongly recommend . . . because . . . ."

State how proposed actions are related to agreed-upon goals and values.
"Since we both want to accomplish the same thing, and we generally hold the same values, I think it would make sense to . . . ."

Invite comment on your analysis.
"Does this make sense to you, or am I missing something?"

When You're a "Third Party" to a Dispute

Sometimes you are asked to help two other parties deal with their disagreements. How can you approach this important — and difficult — task?

- Create a climate for *easy, frank expression* and *thoughtful listening*. During a conflict, the people involved are usually emotional, raising their voices and not listening. By your demeanor, you can help to change this. Your goal is to create a situation in which both parties can speak more rationally and be willing to listen to each other's point of view.

- Model the kind of behavior that you would like to see the participants use. Listen carefully to each party. Look at them when they are speaking.

- Repeat or rephrase what you have heard (e.g. "Let me see if I understand what you have just said . . . .").

- Help the parties to identify where they agree and where they disagree, whether their disagreement is over facts, actions, goals, or values.

- Monitor their listening to one another (e.g.: "Jack, did you understand what Mary just said? How would you express the point she is making?").

- Suggest criteria for evaluating different proposed solutions.

- Underscore areas of agreement.

- Phrase points of agreement and disagreement as accurately and objectively as possible.

- Use every opportunity to applaud the parties for their attitudes, their efforts, and the progress they are making.

- Suggest breaks in the dialogue at appropriate times.

- At the end, summarize what has been accomplished and what steps they might consider next.

The Risks and Rewards of Being Right

When we get into an argument, many of us expend a great deal of effort and energy to prove that we are right.

Why is being "right" so important? (And why is proving that someone else is "wrong" sometimes equally important?)

The Rewards of Being Right	The Risks of Being Right (and Making Someone Else Wrong)
It makes us feel superior.	It may make someone else feel inferior.
We get to do things our way.	Others may do less than their best because they do not like our way.
We feel in control.	The other person may feel powerless.
We avoid being controlled by others.	Others resent being controlled by us.
Our values and beliefs are confirmed.	Other's values and beliefs may be violated.
Victory is sweet.	Defeat is bitter (and may be remembered in future encounters).
We win the argument.	We may lose a relationship.
We win the battle.	We may lose the war.

"Winning" or "losing" in a particular encounter may not be as important as what the *experience* was like for the parties involved — and what was done to nourish or damage their relationship. People with honest differences can maintain a healthy relationship if they show respect and caring as they manage their disputes — and both parties can be enriched, rather than diminished, by the conflict experience.

Creating the Space to Change
(Why Just Being Right Doesn't Work)

It's almost always satisfying to win an argument — to have been proven right, to have defeated an opponent.

How that victory was achieved, however, may be of critical importance.

In a typical conflict, two people are trying to change each other's beliefs or behavior. (The key word is *change*.) Making another person "wrong" does not necessarily make him want to change. A person backed into a corner may feel defeated, may quiet down and may cower — without really changing his mind or his behavior when he gets out of the corner. People need space to change and keep their self-respect and dignity. When cornered, our tendency is to shut down or attack.

We need room to search for a compromise — and we get that room by getting away from the "I'm right — you're wrong" language. "Right–wrong" discussions tend to escalate and deepen the conflict — making it harder for either party to change.

Our choice of words is critical. Language is powerful. Rather than talking in terms of "right" and "wrong," it pays to consider language about "what works" and "what doesn't work" (e.g.: "This doesn't work for me" or "This doesn't work for our department. Does it work for yours?") Concepts like "works" and "doesn't work" are more neutral ways of describing a conflict situation, whereas "right" and "wrong" have moral connotations. Especially in work situations that deal with productivity, timeliness, efficiency, and coordination, it is appropriate to use language like "what works." The goal becomes finding options that "work for both of us."

The Fine Art of Changing Your Mind
with Grace

Sometimes even the smartest of us is wrong. Our knowledge and our experience is limited. Someone else knows something that we have never even thought about.

Sometimes it takes an argument — a conflict — to bring this limitation into focus. Something that we have always believed is challenged. Our natural reaction is to defend what we believe to be true, and to prove that a different view is faulty. The person who disagrees with us is viewed as an opponent to be defeated rather than as one who might teach us something.

We can view such a moment as a contest or as a learning opportunity. Here are some tips for increasing your learning in the midst of a conflict:

- Take a break from the argument. Walk away from the scene. Try to clear your mind and get a fresh start.

- Reexamine both points of view. State as clearly as you can the opposing point of view and the arguments supporting it. (*Do not evaluate.* Just make certain that you have an accurate understanding.)

- Review in your mind why the other party feels so strongly about his or her point of view. What motivations are involved? To what pressures from others might he or she be responding?

- Review in your mind why you feel so strongly about your point of view. What pressures are you responding to?

- If the disagreement is about *facts*, review the actual data or experiences that have been convincing to you. (Even consider the possibility that your memory or perception may be faulty.)

Remember that changing your mind — learning — is not a defeat. It can, in fact, be a sign of maturity and growth.

BIBLIOGRAPHY

DeBono, Edward. *Conflicts: A Better Way to Resolve Them.* London: Harrap Limited, 1985.

Edelman, Joel. *The Tao of Negotiation.* New York: HarperBusiness, 1993.

Fisher, Roger and Scott Brown. *Getting Together.* Boston: Houghton Mifflin, 1988.

Fisher, Roger and William Ury. *Getting to Yes.* Boston: Houghton Mifflin, 1981.

Hanh, Thich Nhat. *Being Peace.* Berkeley, Calif.: Parallax Press, 1987.

Henry, James S., and Jethro K. Lieberman. *The Manager's Guide to Resolving Legal Disputes.* New York: Harper & Row, 1991.

Levine, Stewart. *Getting to Resolution.* San Francisco: Berrett-Koehler, 1998.

Stack, Jack. *The Great Game of Business.* New York: Doubleday, 1992.

Ury, William. *Getting Past No.* New York: Bantam, 1996.

Van Slyke, Erik J. *Listening to Conflict*. New York: AMACOM, 1999.

Weeks, Dudley. *The Eight Essential Steps to Conflict Resolution*. New York: Putnam, 1994.

Weisbord, Marvin R. *Discovering Common Ground*. San Francisco: Berrett-Koehler, 1992.

RECOMMENDED RESOURCES

Assessment Tools and Training Materials

"Dealing with Conflict Instrument" by Alexander Hiam
This new training and development tool incorporates several features that help individuals better understand and enhance their range of conflict-handling techniques. This powerful, yet simple-to-use exercise goes beyond simple self-assessment. It includes a valuable additional exercise (the "Conflict Style Selector") to give individuals the ability to use their own real-life conflicts to test their conflict-handling skills. A rich interpretive section includes a special discussion on the increasing need to use the collaborative skills in both professional and personal settings.

"Dealing with Conflict: 360° Feedback Set" by Alexander Hiam
This includes materials for up to five associates to provide additional insights on the participant's conflict-handling style. Especially useful when people need additional input from others in order to see themselves and their conflict style more clearly.

"Dealing with Conflict Leaders Guide" by Alexander Hiam
This comprehensive guide is the perfect resource for any manager or trainer who is responsible for training individuals and groups on resolving conflict in a constructive manner. Packaged in a three-ring binder, this Leaders Guide includes overhead transparencies, extensive background information for seminar leaders, and a complete participant workbook that can be reproduced for workshops.

Training Videos

Dealing with Conflict (20 minutes)

This popular video demonstrates how pervasive conflict shifts the focus away from work and the basic goals of the team, department, or organization, negatively affecting productivity. The video then offers proven methods for recognizing and resolving confict. The video comes with a clear, practical Leaders Guide.

The Blame Game (10 minutes)

This creative, animated video will help show you and your organization how to start finding solutions, rather than blame. Personal accountability is the answer to the "Blame Game." When managers and employees alike become personally accountable and responsible for their own behaviors and results, everyone benefits. The video comes with a Leaders Guide, handouts for seminars, and two useful, enlightening quizzes.

Attitude Virus: Curing Negativity in the Workplace (21 minutes)

This video demonstrates how bad attitudes spread like viruses through teams, departments, and entire organizations. Productivity suffers, and so do individual workers. From resistance to change, to lack of commitment, to miscommunication, to misdirected anger, attitude virus symptoms can be recognized and reversed. You'll see how to administer the cure for any attitude virus . . . and how to create a healthier workplace for everyone. The video comes with a helpful, practical Leaders Guide.

Training materials and training videos are available from Steps to Success Co. Phone: (323) 227-6205, fax: (323) 227-0705, Web site: www.righttoberight.com.

ABOUT THE AUTHORS

Warren H. Schmidt

Dr. Warren H. Schmidt is professor emeritus of the University of Southern California; president of Chrysalis, Inc., a management training and consulting organization; and chairman of the World Heritage Foundation, an organization dedicated to "sharing and preserving the wonders of our world" through documentary films.

Dr. Schmidt's teaching, writing, and consulting activities are designed to apply social science knowledge to the problems of managing and working in public and private organizations. He is a certified psychologist in California, and a diplomate of the American Board of Professional Psychology.

After teaching psychology at the University of Missouri, Union College, and Springfield College, Dr. Schmidt served in various faculty and administrative positions at UCLA, including director of the unified MBA program and dean of executive education in the graduate school of management. He joined the USC faculty in 1976 as professor of public administration, and was awarded professor emeritus status in 1991.

Dr. Schmidt has been a consultant to both public and private organizations, and a speaker on executive programs throughout the United States and abroad. He chaired the Los Angeles County Economy and Efficiency Commission for several years. He was a member of the Los Angeles City's Quality and Productivity Commission for seven years, and served as its president from 1990 to 1991. He has also served on the Board of Governors for the American Society for Training and Development.

Dr. Schmidt's writings include books, articles, and films. Among his writings is a Harvard Business Review Classic on leadership, cowritten with Robert Tannenbaum. He has screen credits for more than ninety management and educational films, in which he has participated as writer, performer, or advisor. One of the films written by Dr. Schmidt, *Is It Always Right to be Right?*, won an Academy Award in 1971. He has cowritten (with Jerome Finnigan of the Xerox Corporation) two books on total quality management: *The Race Without a Finish Line* and *TQManager*. With Barbara "BJ" Hateley, he is the coauthor of *A Peacock in the Land of Penguins: A Tale of Diversity and Discovery* and *Pigeonholed in the Land of Penguins: A Tale of Seeing beyond Stereotypes*. (Both are available as paperback books and animated videos.) Dr. Schmidt is currently helping to develop a series of television documentary films featuring international "caretakers of culture."

Professor Schmidt's education includes a bachelor's degree from Wayne State University, a master of divinity degree from Concordia Seminary in St. Louis, and an M.A. and Ph.D. in psychology from Washington University.

Dr. Schmidt can be contacted at: Chrysalis, Inc., 9238 Petit Avenue, North Hills, California 91343. Phone: 818-892-3092, fax 818-892-6991.

BJ Gallagher Hateley

BJ Gallagher Hateley is an accomplished management consultant and workshop leader, as well as a popular keynote speaker, specializing in customer service, workforce diversity, innovation and creativity, motivation, teambuilding, leadership skills, personal initiative and accountability, and specialized programs for women.

She is president of her own human resources training and consulting company, Peacock Productions, and has worked with many corporate clients as well as professional associations, nonprofit groups, and government agencies. Her clients include: DaimlerChrysler, Chevron, Tosco, IBM, Nissan, Volkswagen, Southern California Edison, Baxter Health Care, Phoenix Newspapers, Inc., American Lung Association, Planned Parenthood, City of Pasadena, U.S. Immigration & Naturalization Service, American Press Institute, and Certified Grocers of California, among others.

Ms. Gallagher Hateley and Warren H. Schmidt are coauthors of *A Peacock in the Land of Penguins: A Tale of Diversity and Discovery*, which is currently published in twelve languages worldwide, and its sequel, *Pigeonholed in the Land of Penguins: A Tale of Seeing beyond Stereotypes*. She is also coauthor of *What Would Buddha Do at Work?* with Franz Metcalf. Her newest book is *Witty Words from Wise Women: Quips, Quotes, and Comebacks*.

Ms. Gallagher Hateley has worked in the training and adult education field for eighteen years. Before starting her own business in 1991, she served as manager of training and development for the *Los Angeles Times*, where she had key responsibilities in the areas of high-potential leadership development, management assessment and development, workforce diversity, teambuilding, recruitment and selection training, sales training, and customer relations.

Ms. Gallagher Hateley is a Phi Beta Kappa graduate of the University of Southern California, having earned her bachelor's degree summa cum laude in the field of sociology. She has completed the course work for a Ph.D. in social ethics, also at USC.

She has served as a commissioner on the City of Los Angeles Productivity Commission, as a board member for the L. A. chapter of the American Society for Training and Development (ASTD). She is an active member of the National Association of Women Business Owners, the National Speakers Association, and PEN Center USA West.

Ms. Gallagher Hateley can be contacted at: Peacock Productions, 701 Danforth Drive, Los Angeles, California 90065.

Phone: 323-227-6205, fax: 323-227-0705, Web site: www.peacockproductions.com.

Sam Weiss

Sam Weiss has been recognized as one of the preeminent directors in the animation industry for the past twenty-five years. In addition, he brings his unique artistic style to the illustration of books and other print materials, adding character and a charm all his own. He is a versatile artist, film director, musician, and all-round creative spirit.

Sam Weiss has written and/or directed numerous business-oriented training videos, including: *The Winds of Change, To Try Again and Succeed, That's Not My Problem, I Told Them Exactly How to Do It, The Race without a Finish Line, A Peacock in the Land of Penguins* and its sequel, *Pigeonholed in the Land of Penguins.* Other recent productions include: *A Complaint Is a Gift* for Excellence in Training Corporation, *How in Hell Do They Manage?* for CRM Films, and *The Blame Game* for corVision Media.

The films he has directed have been honored all over the world, including an Academy Award nomination for *The Legend of John Henry,* sung by Roberta Flack, and a Television Academy Emmy for *The Wrong Way Kid* (which included four adapted children's books). He has won the Gold Award of the Art Directors Club of New York, Outstanding Film of the Year at the London Film Festival, First Prize at Zagreb International Film Festival, the Jack London Award, and numerous other awards and honors.

Sam Weiss has worked on a number of cartoon series and children's shows. He was art director and designer on the *Mr. Magoo* and *Bullwinkle* shows. He produced and directed *Hot Wheels,* one of the hottest animated series of the late 1960s, as well as thirty-five *G.I. Joe's* for Marvel Productions. He was staff director at Bosustow Entertainment for eleven years, where he directed more than fifty films, including four CBS one-hour specials, which required the adaptation of more than thirty children's books to animation.

During his career Mr. Weiss has directed such voice talents as Carol Burnett, Alan Arkin, Milton Berle, Rob Reiner, Mickey Rooney, Stan Freberg, Patrick Stewart, and many other notable actors and singers.

His education includes studies at the Rhode Island School of Design and the Art Center College of Design.

Sam Weiss can be contacted at: Sam Weiss Productions, 401 Sycamore Road, Santa Monica, California 90402. Phone and fax: 310-459-8838.